# Dollys and Friends
## Originals

Meet Dolly, Polly, Holly, Lolly, Jolly and Molly, new fashion paper dolls Dollys and Friends. You can begin creating your collection of paper dolls with this book which has 3 paper dolls and more than 40 outfits.

Please be aware that these paper dolls require careful hand cutting. For adults, paper dolls may be a gateway to childhood memories but they also make great gifts for children. Younger children may need the help to cut these dolls out since the dolls and clothes are not perforated. However, this is a nice opportunity for fun family time. Paper dolls can bring adults and children together, and collections of paper dolls have always passed down to younger generations. New generations can learn a lot while playing with paper dolls. In a digital era where dress up games allow us to change clothes on paper dolls by only touching a screen, cutting these dolls the traditional way is a great help for developing motor skills. Playing together also helps to develop communication and cooperation between friends and family. Playing games goes hand in hand with storytelling, role-playing and fantasy so everyone can treasure the time spent playing with these paper dolls as memories full of creativity and imagination.

Paper dolls have a long history, and although inspired by antique and vintage paper dolls, Dollys and Friends are modern fashion dolls. Still, most of their wardrobe pieces are vintage fashions or period costumes. While these clothes are created after research, each outfit may not be authentic for that time period. Although there are many costumes and designer fashions for vintage themed books, it is still best to describe them as inspired by historical periods but not exact period costumes. Especially undergarments are more modern for the dolls to be used with different wardrobe choices. Every new outfit from Dollys and Friends Originals Books you will get will be wearable by these Original Dollys. Collecting these paper dolls and sharing them with children can also make fashion and history become one of their passions.

As an illustrator with a background in fashion design, I had hours of fun drawing the Dollys. I really hope that paper doll fans and children of all ages enjoy these creations as much as I did. I wish everyone who is cutting out these dolls and trying the outfits has a great time with this entertaining activity.

Polly

Lolly

Holly

Dolly

Jolly

Molly

by Basak Tinli

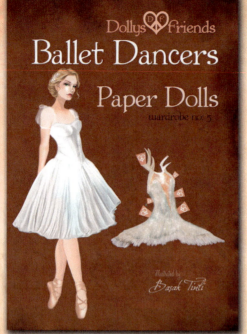
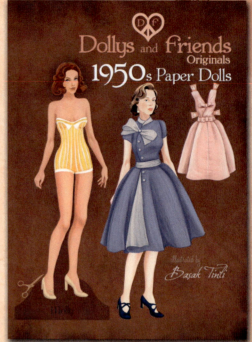
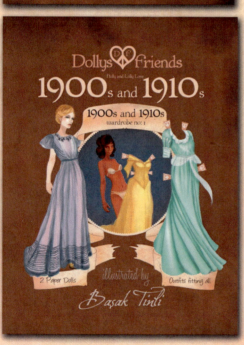
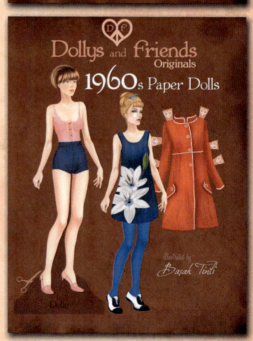

Some Other Wardrobes from the Dollys & Friends
Paper Dolls Series

Please note that only Dollys and Friends Originals Series
have interchangable outfits.

All illustrations by Basak Tinli. Please do not copy and/or reproduce the
artwork in any form. No part of this book may be reproduced,
distributed, or transmitted by any means
without the permission of the publisher.
All rights reserved.

Made in the USA
Middletown, DE
19 October 2022